The Story of the

LITTLE ROCK NINE

AND SCHOOL DESEGREGATION

in Photographs

David Aretha

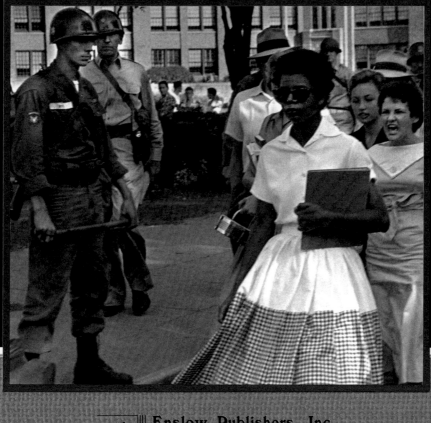

 Enslow Publishers, Inc.
40 Industrial Road
Box 398
Berkeley Heights, NJ 07922
USA
http://www.enslow.com

Library of Congress Cataloging-in-Publication Data

Aretha, David.

The story of the Little Rock nine and school desegregation in photographs / David Aretha.
    pages cm. — (The story of the Civil Rights Movement in photographs)
Includes index.
Summary: "Discusses the desegregation of Little Rock Central High School, including the nine African-American students that successfully integrated the Arkansas school and the controversy and crisis surrounding the event"—Provided by publisher.
ISBN 978-0-7660-4235-3
    1. School integration—Arkansas—Little Rock—History—20th century—Pictorial work—Juvenile literature. 2. Central High School (Little Rock, Ark.)—History—20th century—Pictorial work—Juvenile literature. 3. African American high school students—Arkansas—Little Rock—History—20th century—Pictorial work—Juvenile literature. I. Title.
LC214.23.L56A74 2014
379.2'630976773—dc23

2012041371

Future editions:
Paperback ISBN: 978-1-4644-0413-9   EPUB ISBN: 978-1-4645-1226-1
Singler-User PDF ISBN: 978-1-4646-1226-8   Multi-User PDF ISBN: 978-0-7660-5858-3

Printed in the United States of America
112013 Bang Printing, Brainerd, Minn.
10 9 8 7 6 5 4 3 2 1

To Our Readers: We have done our best to make sure all Internet Addresses in this book were active and appropriate when we went to press. However, the author and the publisher have no control over and assume no liability for the material available on those Internet sites or on other Web sites they may link to. Any comments or suggestions can be sent by e-mail to comments@enslow.com or to the address on the back cover.

♻ Enslow Publishers, Inc., is committed to printing our books on recycled paper. The paper in every book contains 10% to 30% post-consumer waste (PCW). The cover board on the outside of each book contains 100% PCW. Our goal is to do our part to help young people and the environment too!

Illustration Credits: AP Images, pp. 4, 11, 16, 27, 30, 39; AP Images / BK, p. 35; AP Images / Corbis Bettman, pp. 18–19, 28; AP Images / FJG, pp. 2, 22 (top and bottom); AP Images / lr, p. 37; AP Images/ Will Counts, p. 43; AP Images / William J. Smith, pp. 24, 42; AP Images / William P. Straeter, pp. 3, 10, 20, 36; Library of Congress Prints and Photographs, pp. 8–9, 12, 40 (top and bottom); Little Rock Central High School National Historic Site, p. 37 (diploma); Lloyd Dinkins / The Commercial Appeal / Landov, pp. 1, 14; Will Counts Collection: Indiana University Archives, pp. 17, 33.

Cover Illustration: Lloyd Dinkins / The Commercial Appeal / Landov (Elizabeth Ann Eckford denied entrance to Little Rock Central High School on September 4, 1957).

Table of Contents

Lawyers George E. C. Hayes, Thurgood Marshall, and James M. Nabrit (left to right) celebrate their great victory in front of the U.S. Supreme Court Building. On May 17, 1954, the court ruled that segregation would no longer be tolerated in America's public schools.

Introduction

n the United States of America, all citizens have the right to free education in public schools. Unfortunately, free education has not always meant equal education.

For a hundred years after slavery was abolished in 1865, the southern United States was largely segregated. A segregated society means that the dominant racial group separates and mistreats a less-powerful group. Southern white people dominated politics in their states. They created laws favorable to whites and unfair to African Americans. In the segregated South, whites had separate and better facilities. Among many other establishments, white schools, restaurants, churches, and theaters were superior to those built for black citizens.

Pauli Murray grew up in North Carolina. She wrote in her 1956 book *Proud Shoes*: "Our seedy run-down school told us that if we had any place at all in the grand scheme of things it was a separate place. . . . We were bottled up and labeled and sent aside—sent to the [segregated] car, the back of the bus, the side door of the theater, the side window of a restaurant. We came to know that whatever we had was always inferior."

For generations, African Americans were not able to challenge the system. Whites in the South kept them poor by paying low wages. They created schemes to prevent most black citizens from voting. Law enforcement and hate groups, such as the Ku Klux Klan, intimidated any black people who "stepped out of line." Up through the 1950s, the U.S. government rarely came to the aid of southern African Americans.

When it came to segregation, the saddest discrepancies were in the public schools. White students went to decent schools. No black students were allowed to attend them. Black students were assigned to inferior "colored" schools. In 1940, some states in the South spent more than twice as much money on each white student as they did on each black pupil.

In Mississippi, the state spent $513 per white student and just $89 for each black student.

In 1933, black lawyers Thurgood Marshall and Charles Houston toured the South to review the black and white schools. They found that the white school in one southern county had "six rooms, six teachers. Assembly hall, piano, individual desks. Three buses to transport children." The black school in the county had "68 pupils packed into one room, 20 × 16 feet, on seven benches. No tables, no desks, no stove [for heating]. One chair, one open fireplace." When black children had to use the bathroom, they had to "cross railroad and highway to get to the woods."

For years, Houston and Marshall fought against segregation in federal (U.S.) courts. They argued that segregated schools violated the rights of African Americans. The U.S. Constitution, they pointed out, promised equal rights for all Americans. In their many court cases, Houston and Marshall proved that schools for black students were inferior. In addition, the concept of separate schools for black children was unfair. Psychologists took the witness stand. They stated that black students felt unwanted by white society. They felt inferior.

On May 17, 1954, the U.S. Supreme Court made a historic ruling in the case *Brown v. Board of Education of Topeka Kansas*. In that case, Marshall argued that segregated public schools should be abolished. The Supreme Court agreed. "We conclude," Chief Justice Earl Warren declared, "that in the field of public education the doctrine of 'separate but equal' has no place. Separate educational facilities are inherently unequal."

From that point forward, segregated schools violated federal law. The next year, the Supreme Court ruled that segregated schools had to be desegregated. White schools had to admit black students. But the Supreme Court ruled that the desegregation process should occur "with all deliberate speed." That phrase, though, was vague. *Deliberate* can be understood as being slow. And that's how southern politicians considered it.

The majority of southern white citizens did not want to desegregate the schools. They didn't want their children learning with, befriending, or dating black students. So, as the editor of one newsletter stated, the southern strategy on desegregation "was to delay, delay, delay."

In 1956, 101 members of Congress signed a document called the "Southern Manifesto." They announced that their states would refuse to obey the Supreme Court's decision. By 1957, few of the South's white schools had opened their doors to black students.

However, the school board in Little Rock, Arkansas, was willing to gradually integrate its schools. School board members agreed that Central High School would be the first to integrate, beginning in September 1957. The federal district court agreed with the school board and insisted on integration.

Daisy Bates, an African-American civil rights activist in Little Rock, took the lead. "The time for delay, evasion, or procrastination was over," she declared. The school board selected ten black students to desegregate Central High School. One student chose not to enroll. The rest became the "Little Rock Nine"—all excellent students from respected families. They also were considered mature enough to deal with the publicity and harassment they might face.

Many whites in Little Rock remained strongly opposed to integration. On August 27, 1957, the all-white Mother's League of Central High School held its first public meeting. They also filed a motion in local court to prevent the Little Rock Nine from attending Central High School. On August 29, the court sided with the Mother's League.

The first day of classes at Central High would be September 4. Would the Little Rock Nine students show up that day? Would they be admitted into the school? Many expected a conflict. But few could have dreamed that the president would need to call in the U.S. Army.

Chapter 1

CRISIS
in Little Rock

The Integration Decision

Little Rock is the capital of Arkansas. It has long been the state's largest city. In 1957, its population was slightly more than 100,000. Typical for a southern city, its schools were segregated. In 1955, however, the Little Rock school board members were ready to change that. They voted to allow African-American students into white schools beginning in 1957. Little Rock Central High School would be the first school to integrate. However, most white citizens in Little Rock strongly opposed this idea.

Black and white citizens stroll through downtown Little Rock, Arkansas. Little Rock was not as segregated as other southern cities. By the mid-1950s, the buses, parks, and libraries had all been integrated. Schools, however, were a different story.

Daisy Bates (left) shares a smile with fellow civil rights activist Clarence Laws. Bates was the leader of the school-integration movement in Little Rock.

Bates Leads the Way

Why did the Little Rock school board vote to integrate Central High School? Largely because of Daisy Bates. She was president of the Arkansas NAACP (National Association for the Advancement of Colored People). For years, Bates condemned segregation while writing for the *Arkansas State Press*, a newspaper that her husband published. In that newspaper, she declared that she would challenge the Little Rock school board to integrate the city's schools. "So the reason that they put together this plan," Ernest Green told *National Public Radio* writer Juan Williams in 2007, "was because Daisy forced them to put the plan together."

Faubus Flip-Flops

Prior to 1957, Arkansas governor Orval Faubus was sympathetic to African Americans. He had ended segregation on the state's buses, and he was working toward school integration. However, as the integration of Central High School loomed closer, Arkansas politicians urged Faubus to take a stand against it. He did, largely because he wanted to remain popular with white voters. Under the governor's direction, the Arkansas National Guard prevented black students from entering Central High on September 4, 1957.

Arkansas Governor Orval Faubus said the U.S. Supreme Court should "keep its cotton-picking hands off the Little Rock School Board's affairs." In this photo, he displays a newspaper (dated September 3) with the headline "Anger and Threats Mar School Opening."

The Little Rock Nine pose with Daisy Bates. Standing (left to right) are Ernest Green, Melba Pattillo, Terrance Roberts, Carlotta Walls, Bates, and Jefferson Thomas. Seated (left to right) are Thelma Mothershed, Minnijean Brown, Elizabeth Eckford, and Gloria Ray.

From Seventy-Five to Nine

The Little Rock school board voted to integrate its schools, beginning with Central High. However, most whites in the state did not want integration. One poll indicated that 85 percent of Arkansans opposed the integration of their learning facilities. School board members started getting nervous. They feared that integration might cause turmoil.

Seventy-five African-American students wanted to attend Central High. That was too many, the school board members believed. The fewer the black students, they thought, the less opposition there would be. The school board officials pared the number down to twenty-five. Then they tried to convince at least some of the twenty-five students not to come to the school. Recalled the NAACP's Wiley Branton in the book *Eyes on the Prize*: "[They] began calling parents of kids, saying, 'If you really want your son to play football, you ought to stay over there at Horace Mann [the all-black school].'"

In the end, the school board admitted only ten (including Jane Hill, who chose not to attend after September 4) of the twenty-five. Those chosen were all fine students from well-regarded families. The board selected them, Branton said, "because they were trying to get 'good' Negroes. . . . They became the Little Rock Nine and carved out a place in history."

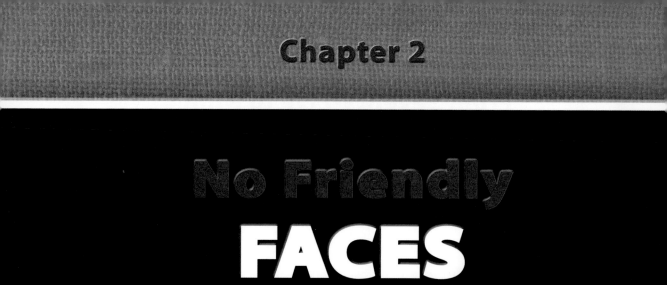

Chapter 2

No Friendly FACES

Here Comes the National Guard

On September 3, 1957, federal (U.S.) judge Ronald Davies ruled that Central High School integrate the following day. For African Americans in Little Rock, it should have been a reason to celebrate. However, Governor Orval Faubus defied the judge's order. On September 3, Faubus announced that the Arkansas National Guard would be at Central High the next morning. Armed with rifles, they would prevent the African-American students from entering the school. Many whites in the city cheered the decision. Meanwhile, African-American citizens feared for the safety of the ten black students.

Hostile whites threatened Elizabeth Ann Eckford when she showed up for her first day of school. "I tried to see a friendly face somewhere in the mob," she wrote in *The Long Shadow of Little Rock*. But she didn't. Instead, someone yelled, "Get out of here!" In this photo, Hazel Bryan (now Hazel Massery) yells slurs at Eckford.

A young man displays the Confederate flag in front of Central High School. The flag had symbolized the South's resistance to the U.S. government during the Civil War.

Eckford Goes It Alone

Though she knew the National Guard would be at the school, Daisy Bates did not back down. On September 3, she made arrangements with the black students. She told them that she would meet them all the next morning. Together, they would try to enter Central High's rear entrance. However, the Eckford family did not have a telephone. Elizabeth never got Bates's message. Elizabeth arrived at the front of the school—by herself.

"Lynch Her! Lynch Her!"

The armed National Guardsmen were enough to frighten fifteen-year-old Elizabeth Eckford. "They glared at me with a mean look," she recalled in *The Long Shadow of Little Rock*. But much scarier was a gathering of hundreds of hostile whites. They chanted, "Two, four, six, eight, we ain't gonna integrate." The mob surrounded Elizabeth and threatened her. "They moved closer and closer," she recalled. "Somebody started yelling, 'Lynch her! Lynch her!'" An older white woman, she said, spat on her face.

A National Guardsman prevents Little Rock Nine students from entering Central High on September 4.

On September 4, National Guardsmen prevented Elizabeth Eckford from entering the school. They then failed to protect her when she became engulfed by a white mob.

Six African-American students attempted to integrate North Little Rock High School on September 9, 1957. School officials did not admit the students, but the principal agreed to meet with the six boys. White students, however, refused to let them in the school.

Chapter 3

Calling in the U.S. ARMY

The Nine's Short School Day

On September 20, 1957, Judge Davies ordered Governor Faubus to remove the Arkansas National Guard from Little Rock Central High School. This time, the governor agreed to the order. On Monday, September 23, Daisy Bates led the Little Rock Nine back to Central High. The National Guard was no longer there. Mayor Woodrow Mann had indicated that police officers would protect the students. But after the Little Rock Nine entered the school, a large group of whites gathered outside the building. Because of the hostile crowd, Mayor Mann felt that the students were in danger. Shortly after noon, police escorted the students to their homes.

Angry whites shove Alex Wilson near Central High School on September 23, 1957. Wilson was a reporter from the *Tri-State Defender*, a newspaper based in Memphis, Tennessee. Segregationists were often hostile to African-American reporters as well as white reporters from the North.

Eisenhower Calls in the Troops

On September 23, 1957, President Dwight Eisenhower became deeply involved in the Little Rock crisis. He knew that the rulings of the U.S. judges and courts had to be enforced. That day, the president ordered Central High School's white protesters to "cease and desist." He hoped that this order would put an end to the mobs that had gathered at the school.

On the morning of September 24, the Nine did not try to go to school. However, another white mob gathered there. Eisenhower, the heroic general of World War II, took further action. He ordered 1,000 troops of the 101st Airborne Division into Little Rock. On the 24th, these soldiers were stationed all around the school. Many local whites felt that their city had been invaded by the U.S. Army.

In addition, Eisenhower federalized the Arkansas National Guard. This meant that the National Guard members no longer took orders from Governor Faubus. They now were required to take orders from the president. National Guardsmen would be sent to Central High. But instead of preventing the Little Rock Nine from entering the school—like they had in early September—the National Guardsmen would protect them.

At a press conference, President Dwight Eisenhower answers questions about the Little Rock crisis.

The President Addresses the Nation

President Eisenhower continued to address the Little Rock situation. On September 24, he went on television and explained to Americans why he had sent in troops. "We are a nation in which laws, not men, are supreme...," he said. "Mob rule cannot be allowed to override the decisions of our courts." He also said that the crisis had become an embarrassment to the United States. "Our enemies are gloating over this incident, using it everywhere to misrepresent our whole nation."

Eisenhower's address was unusual. Few presidents had ever shown public support for African-American rights. Eisenhower himself rarely seemed to care much. In his eight years as president, this was his only major civil rights speech.

The president's use of force in Little Rock angered many southern politicians. Mississippi senator James Eastland said it was "an attempt to destroy the social order of the South." But Eisenhower did not back down. The next morning, on September 25, the Little Rock Nine would attend Central High School. The U.S. Army would escort them into the school—and no one was going to stop them.

Through the Doors of
CENTRAL HIGH

An Army Escort

On the morning of September 25, a station wagon and two jeeps pulled up in front of Central High School. The wagon carried the Little Rock Nine. The jeeps carried army troops. All the while, armed soldiers lined the school. Helicopters hovered above. At around 9:30 A.M., twenty-two soldiers escorted the African-American teens through the front door.

In the book *Voices of Freedom*, Melba Pattillo recalled: "[T]here was a feeling of pride and hope that yes, this is the United States; yes, there is a reason I salute the flag; and it's going to be okay."

Top: Troops escort the Little Rock Nine into Central High on September 26, their second day of classes. **Bottom:** The troops were under orders to clear away protesters from the school. Here, they march white students down the block.

Jefferson Thomas and Elizabeth Eckford eat lunch in the school cafeteria. White students were rarely friendly with the Little Rock Nine—and sometimes hostile toward them.

"Am I Less Than Human?"

On September 25, General Edwin Walker addressed all of Central High's students. He said that any student who was disruptive would be "removed by the soldiers on duty and turned over to the local police." Members of the National Guard remained in the school throughout the year, protecting the Little Rock Nine. Melba Pattillo was glad they were there. "They were wonderful, they were disciplined, they were attentive, they were caring," she said in *Voices of Freedom*.

Daisy Bates also provided continuous support. "We would meet at [Bates's] house every morning," Thelma Mothershed said in *Voices of Freedom*, "then we'd go back there in the evening for our parents to pick us up."

Most of the teachers were courteous to the nine black students. Most white students left them alone, but some bullied them severely. Whites destroyed their lockers, hit them, and stepped on their heels. They threw flaming wads of paper at the black students, and they flung lighted sticks of dynamite at them. One student broke a bottle on the volleyball court and tripped Pattillo. "I have scars on my right knee from that," she said. "After a while, I started saying to myself, Am I less than human? Why did they do this to me?"

A white student punches a dummy of a black student near Central High School on October 3, 1957. This incident occurred on the day that white students walked out of the school in protest of integration.

Harassed and Abused

Tensions in Central High School continued for weeks and months. In early October, several dozen white students protested integration by walking out of their school. They hoped that hundreds of students would join them. When they didn't, they vented their frustrations in another way. They made a black dummy and hanged it from a tree. This mimicked a lynching. Over the previous century, whites had lynched several thousand African Americans in a similar way. Most of these lynchings occurred in the South.

White students continued to physically abuse the Little Rock Nine. Melba Pattillo said that whites often turned off the cold water in their locker-room showers. The hot water would remain on, burning their skin. On another occasion, a student threw a chemical into her eyes, causing them to burn. A friend immediately splashed water into her eyes. If he hadn't, an eye doctor said, she might have gone blind.

A student named Andy often harassed Pattillo. One time, he slashed a knife at her. It cut through the cover of the book she used to protect herself. Melba said she had to become a warrior. "I had to learn," she later told *CNN*, ". . . how to get from that door to the end of the hall without dying."

Chapter 5

RETALIATION and GRADUATION

"I Want to Go Home"

For many at Central High School, the 1957–1958 school year was long and difficult. Many whites remained troubled that their "southern way of life" was changing. Of course, the nine African-American students suffered the most. One day in October, Elizabeth Eckford entered the office of Vice Principal Elizabeth Huckaby. Eckford had been crying. "I want to go home," she said, as recounted in the book *Eyes on the Prize*. Huckaby said that the Little Rock Nine couldn't give up. To do so would be a setback for school integration. "I finally persuaded Elizabeth to stay and walked with her to her history class," Huckaby said.

Minnijean Brown stands among white students outside the school in October 1957. The school had been evacuated because of a bomb threat.

Minnijean Brown Strikes Back

Daisy Bates instructed the Little Rock Nine to always be on their best behavior. But in the cafeteria on December 17, Minnijean Brown couldn't take it anymore. A white boy, who was much smaller than her, continually harassed her. In *Voices of Freedom*, Ernest Green recalled what happened. Minnijean took a bowl of chili "and dumped it on this dude's head," Green said. "There was absolute silence in the place, and then the help [cafeteria workers], all black, broke into applause. And the white kids . . . didn't know what to do. It was the first time that anybody, I'm sure, had seen somebody black retaliate in that sense."

In February, a white girl called Brown a terrible name. She responded by calling the white girl a name. For *her* misconduct, Minnijean was expelled from the school. Historian Taylor Branch pointed out how unfairly the black students were treated. "These people had to endure torment and respond with perfect behavior," he said.

After Brown was expelled, smart-aleck white students made up cards that said, "One down, eight to go!" But no more black students would be expelled. As for Minnijean, she went to New York to finish high school.

Daisy Bates was like a second mother to the Little Rock Nine. Here, Daisy and her husband, L.C., host a pre-Thanksgiving dinner for the students in 1957.

When Minnijean Brown (center) was expelled, Thelma Mothershed (right) had one less friend at Central High. Thelma endured her own humiliations. One teacher assigned her a seat and made sure that the desks behind her were empty. She didn't want to make white students sit behind a black girl. She didn't want to hurt *their* feelings.

Ernest Green's Graduation

Anger simmered at Central all the way to graduation day on May 29, 1958. Ernest Green was the only senior among the Little Rock Nine. He graduated along with 601 white students. In her book, *Warriors Don't Cry*, Melba Pattillo recalled a white student saying: "You'all think you're gonna have a graduation, but a funeral is what you're really gonna have."

When Green walked on stage to receive his diploma, whites in the audience refused to clap. However, he had the support of his family, as well as Martin Luther King, Jr., who showed up for this historic event. Green recalled in the documentary, *Eyes on the Prize*: "I knew I was walking for the other eight students that were there. I figured I was making a statement and helping black people's existence in Little Rock. . . . I knew that once I got as far as that principal and received that diploma, I had cracked the wall."

Ernest Green beamed with pride when he received his diploma—even though whites responded with silence.

Chapter 6

"THE LOST YEAR"
and Beyond

Faubus Closes the High Schools

By fighting against integration, Governor Orval Faubus became hugely popular among southern whites. In September 1958, Faubus took an extreme action. He ordered that all four public high schools in Little Rock be closed. He promised to make them private schools. If the schools were private, he said, the U.S. government couldn't force them to accept African Americans. He was wrong; courts did not allow him to "privatize" public schools. Thus, Little Rock was left with four closed high schools for eleven months. It was known as "The Lost Year."

Vote against
Integration!

After Governor Faubus decided to close Little Rock's public high schools, the city's citizens got to vote on the matter. Here, white Central High students support the governor's decision during a pro-segregation rally outside the capitol. The majority of the voters also supported their governor.

The four Little Rock high schools were closed for the 1958–1959 school year. Most of the white students were educated in other schools. For a few weeks, the school district educated students through television. This boy learns in his pajamas.

During "The Lost Year," no private schools were available for black students. This African American attempts to learn something from a teacher on television. However, about half of the black students did no academic work at all that year.

Black Students Suffer the Most

The closure of Little Rock's high schools changed many lives. For the 1958–1959 school year, about half of the city's white students enrolled in private schools. About one-third of the white students attended schools in other cities. More than six hundred white teens did not attend any school at all. As for African Americans, most of them did not go to school that year.

The U.S. Supreme Court reviewed the Little Rock case. The justices determined that the closing of Little Rock's high schools was unconstitutional. That means it violated the U.S. Constitution; it was against the law. On August 12, 1959, Little Rock's public high schools would reopen. They would include white students and a small number of black students—including four members of the Little Rock Nine.

Whites in Little Rock were still angry about this disruption in their lives. In August, white mobs again harassed black students as they entered the public schools. One of the students' houses was bombed. However, local police protected the black students. Forevermore, Little Rock's schools would be integrated.

On August 26, 1958, Daisy Bates and the Little Rock Nine visited the Lincoln Memorial in Washington, D.C. Lincoln may have "freed the slaves" in 1863, but ninety-five years later, African Americans still weren't truly free.

In September 1997, Elizabeth Eckford talks with Hazel Massery. On page 14 of this book, Massery is pictured heckling Eckford. An older and wiser Massery apologized for her actions. She and Eckford became friends.

Learning to Live Together

The integration of Central High was a new experience for everyone. Whites had grown up thinking that they were superior to African Americans. The integration made them angry. The change made them fearful. Dent Gitchel was the student who provoked Minnijean Brown, prompting her to dump chili on his head. In *USA Today* in 2007, Gitchel recalled his thought patterns in 1957. "All this stuff was swirling around me," he said. "I was bewildered by what was going on." He added that 1957 was "the year I really started thinking." Over time, whites in Little Rock realized that African Americans were their equals, and they truly could live together.

Over time, racial tensions eased in Little Rock's high schools. White students still tended to hang out with whites—and black students with blacks. But the two groups learned to accept one another. Many white and black students became friends. In 1982, the *Los Angeles Times* claimed that Central High School was the best school in Arkansas. At that time, about half of the school's students were African American.

Sadly, many cities endured growing pains similar to Little Rock's. In the 1950s and 1960s, communities throughout the South rebelled against forced school integration. In Clinton, Tennessee, those who opposed integration bombed the high school. In 1963, citizens in Alabama protested when a federal court ordered Alabama schools to integrate. In Prince Edward County, Virginia, the local government closed the public schools in 1959. They kept them closed for five years!

Even when schools integrated, only a small number of African Americans enrolled in them. For decades—up to the present day—the racial makeup of public schools has been an issue throughout the United States. Most black students still go to schools that are mostly African American. These schools tend to be in poorer neighborhoods, and the students often receive a weaker education. In the 1960s, 1970s, and beyond, efforts were made to bus black students to white schools. However, most Americans opposed "busing." It was considered a failed experiment.

On a brighter note, the Little Rock Nine turned into a fabulous success story. Every single one of the nine students enjoyed a fruitful career.

Ernest Green served as Assistant Secretary of Housing and Urban Affairs under President Jimmy Carter. Elizabeth Eckford became a social worker and raised two sons. Terrence Roberts became a psychologist. Jefferson Thomas was an accountant. Carlotta Walls graduated from Michigan State University and worked in real estate. Minnijean Brown became a writer and social worker. Gloria Ray was a successful magazine publisher. Thelma Mothershed became a teacher. And Melba Pattillo was a journalist for NBC.

September 1997 marked the fortieth anniversary of the Little Rock crisis. Each of the Little Rock Nine members returned to Central High School for the anniversary ceremony. So, too, did President Bill Clinton, who had grown up in Arkansas. In a symbolic gesture, the president opened the front door for these former students. "It was Little Rock," he said, "that made racial equality a driving obsession in my life."

Clinton shook each of the Little Rock Nine's hands. In a passionate speech, he honored them for their incredible bravery. "Forty years ago, they climbed these steps, passed through this door, and moved our nation," Clinton said. "For that, we must all thank them."

Two years later, the Little Rock Nine earned Congressional Gold Medals. Again, President Clinton led the ceremony. He delivered an emotional speech and handed out the medals. Clinton had a particular soft spot for Elizabeth Eckford. He had seen the old photos of her from September 4, 1957. He remembered her being alone, surrounded by a mob, heckled, and spat upon.

"Come here, girl," Clinton said to Eckford. The president gave her not just a medal, but a very long hug.

1865–1965: After slavery, African Americans in the South are confined to segregated (separate, inferior) facilities. They are denied other citizenship rights, such as voting.

1954: The U.S. Supreme Court bans segregation in public schools.

1955–56: Martin Luther King, Jr., leads a successful yearlong boycott of segregated buses in Montgomery, Alabama.

1957: The National Guard helps black students integrate Central High School in Little Rock, Arkansas.

1960–mid-1960s: Civil rights activists stage hundreds of sit-ins at segregated restaurants, stores, theaters, libraries, and many other establishments.

1961: Activists stage Freedom Rides on segregated buses in the South.

1963: Thousands of African Americans protest segregation in Birmingham, Alabama.

1963: A quarter-million Americans attend the March on Washington for Jobs and Freedom in Washington, D.C.

1964: Activists register black voters in Mississippi during "Freedom Summer."

1964: The U.S. Congress passes the Civil Rights Act. It outlaws segregation and other racial injustices.

1965: African Americans protest voting injustice in Selma, Alabama.

1965: Congress passes the Voting Rights Act, which guarantees voting rights for all Americans.

Further Reading

Books

Bates, Daisy. *The Long Shadow of Little Rock: A Memoir.* Fayetteville, Ark.: University of Arkansas Press, 1986.

Beals, Melba Pattillo. *Warriors Don't Cry: The Searing Memoir of the Battle to Integrate Little Rock's Central High.* New York: Simon Pulse, 2007.

Jacoway, Elizabeth. *Turn Away Thy Son: Little Rock, the Crisis That Shook the Nation.* New York: Free Press, 2007.

Tougas, Shelley. *Little Rock Girl 1957: How a Photograph Changed the Fight for Integration.* Mankato, Minn.: Compass Point Books, 2012.

Walker, Paul Robert. *Remember Little Rock: The Time, the People, the Stories.* Washington, D.C.: National Geographic, 2009.

Internet Addresses

Little Rock Nine Foundation
<http://littlerock9.com/>

Southern School Desegregation: 1957–1962
<http://www.pbs.org/wgbh/
amex/eyesontheprize/story/
02_schools.html>

Index